How to Make
ELEPHANT BREAD

by Kathy Mandry and Joe Toto

Pantheon Books

To Maria,
   Michael,
   Melissa
and Martin

How to Make Elephant Bread

Grownups have fancy names for the foods they eat.
They call beef stew Beef Stroganoff,
and chunks of meat on a stick, Shishkebab.
And there are a lot more too.
But what about boys and girls?
Nobody gives them fancy names for
the foods they eat.
A banana is called a banana.
A glass of milk is a glass of milk.
A peanut butter sandwich is
a peanut butter sandwich.
But if chunks of meat on a stick
can be Shishkebab,
why can't a peanut butter sandwich be
Elephant Bread?

Elephant Bread

Take a slice of bread and
spread some peanut butter on it
with a spoon.
Then take another slice of bread
and cover the peanut butter up.
If you can't find an
elephant who wants it,
eat it yourself.

Jungle Juice

Pour yourself half a glass of
pineapple juice.
Then fill up the rest of
the glass with orange juice.
If you can find a cherry,
drop one in.
Stir it all up with a spoon.
If you listen very carefully,
you can hear
the whole jungle roar.

Spooky Cream

Put a big scoop of
vanilla ice cream in a dish.
Stick four marshmallows
on top of the ice cream.
If you can find some coconut,
sprinkle that on top too.
If it tries to scare you,
don't run away or it will melt.

Tree Trunk

Put a slice of bologna
on a plate.
Then put a slice of
cheese on top.
Roll them up together.
Before you eat it, make sure
no squirrels are hiding inside.

Drink a Garden

Pour yourself a glass
of tomato juice.
Wash a small stalk of celery,
one red radish,
and the tip of a carrot.
Sprinkle a little salt
in the juice.
Take a sip, eat some radish.
Take another sip, eat some carrot.
Take another sip, eat some celery.
Keep going until it's all gone.
If you find the gardener's tools
at the bottom, give them back.

Apple Swamp

Put some applesauce in a dish.
Throw in a handful of raisins
and a handful of nuts.
Stir them all up with a spoon.
Eat them before they swim away.

Bunny Stick

Take a whole carrot.
Wash it.
Then wash a big leaf of lettuce
and wrap it around the carrot.
Put some salt on it before
you take the first bite.
Don't crunch too loudly
or you'll wake up all the bunnies.

Chocolate Cat

Pour some milk into a big glass.
Get a spoonful of chocolate.
Put it in the milk and
stir it all up with the spoon.
If a cat who likes chocolate
wants some, don't give him any.
Drink it yourself.

Eat a Sunset

Peel an orange very carefully.
Separate each section and
put them on a dish.
Sprinkle some cinnamon
and sugar on top.
Then eat each section with
your fingers.
If it gets too bright,
wear sunglasses.

Barnyard Hero

Get a plate.
Put a slice of bread on it.
Take two slices of ham and
put them on top of the bread.
Cover it with another slice
of bread.
Put one slice of cheese and
one lettuce leaf on top of that.
Then take another slice
of bread and cover it all up.
If it puts up a fight, bite it.

Bumbleberry Shake

Find an empty jar with a cover.
Make sure it's clean.
Pour a glass of milk in it.
Put in a spoonful of honey
and a little strawberry syrup.
Screw the lid on tight and
shake with all your might
until you see bubbles.
Then pour it into your glass
and drink it.
If you bumble,
don't let it shake you up.

Bear Berries

Put some blueberries in a bowl.
Pour two spoonfuls of honey on
top of the berries and then a
little bit of milk.
If a grizzly bear wants them,
tell him to go pick his own.

Snow on the Roof

Put a graham cracker on a dish.
Spread strawberry jam on it.
Put another graham cracker on top.
Spread it with raspberry jam.
Put one last graham cracker
on top of that.
Then put a scoop of vanilla
ice cream on top of it all.
Wait a few minutes until
the ice cream makes
the crackers soft.
Then finish it fast,
before the roof caves in.

Monkey Business

Take a banana.
Peel it halfway with
your fingers and let the
peels hang down.
Then pour some chocolate syrup
into a dish.
Dip the banana in
and take a bite.
Keep going until you finish.
But watch out for
monkeys with long arms.
Especially near trees.

Bubble Up Bright

Put two ice cubes in a glass.
Fill it halfway
with ginger ale.
Then fill the other half
with orange juice.
Throw a cherry in.
If the bubbles
hit you in the nose,
hit them back.